Gratitude
A 40 Day Adventure

Vicki Andree

"Scripture quotations are from The ESV® Bible (The Holy Bible, English Standard Version®), copyright © 2001 by Crossway, a publishing ministry of Good News Publishers. Used by permission. All rights reserved."

Copyright © 2019 Vicki Andree

All rights reserved.

ISBN: 109272365X
ISBN-13: 9781092723657

Table of Contents

Table of Contents 1
Gratitude 2
The Lord Provides 3
He Quiets Me 4
He Chooses The Time 5
He Renews My Strength 6
He Restores Me 7
He Delights Me 8
His Mysterious Ways 9
He Protects Me 10
He Lifts Me Up 11
His Abundance 12
He Rejoices Over Me 13
He Surrounds Me 14
His Desire For Me 15
He Fights For Me 16
He Promised 17
He Cultivates Me 18
He Walks With Me 19
He Bestows Wisdom 20
He Arranges Divine Appointments 21
He Increases My Days 22
He Feeds Me 23
His Peace Shields Me 24
He Calms My Storms 25
He Fulfills The Impossible 26
He Increases My Faith 27
He Forgives Me 28
He Frees Me 29
He Keeps Me Forever 30
He Is Love 31
He Offers Me The Kingdom 32
His Power Overcomes 33
He Offers New Life 34
His Incredible Fruit 35
He Satisfies 36
His Grace 37
He Encourages Me 38
He Focuses On My Future 39
He Teaches Me 40
He Completes Me 41
He Is Greater 42
Conclusion 43
Books by Vicki Andree 44

Gratitude

Dear Reader,
You may not consider gratitude an activity, but I can personally testify that it is! As I strive to serve the Creator and Sustainer of the universe every day of my life, I find it impossible not to experience gratitude for His provision in all things.

The activity of gratitude takes place in your mind where battles are won and lost. No matter what you are facing, gratitude will always give you an edge.

Writing a few words in this journal will increase your awareness of your spiritual involvement with, and subsequent provisions, from God. Just acknowledging three things a day that you are grateful for can change your attitude. Before you start writing, let me tell you about some of the incredible benefits of having a grateful attitude.

A grateful attitude can change your heart. This new attitude can actually draw you closer to the LORD. Consider how a new, deeper walk with God can change your life, and for those around you.

Gratitude can reduce depression as your spirits soars while expressing your grateful heart to our Savior. Grateful people are humble people. Humility is one attribute God requires of each believer. Humility cannot be achieved without gratitude.

Gratitude then leads to contentment. When you are grateful for what you have, where you are in life, you have no reason to complain. You will sleep better knowing God is in control and that He loves you more than you can ever comprehend.

One study claims that patients who counted their blessings once a week actually lowered their blood pressure. Just think what once a day could do!

These are but a few of the many benefits of a grateful heart. My prayer is that you will spend the next forty days thanking God for His many benefits as you grow more optimistic, less materialistic, healthier, less competitive, relaxed, happier, and well rested. May the LORD continue to bless you!

The Lord Provides

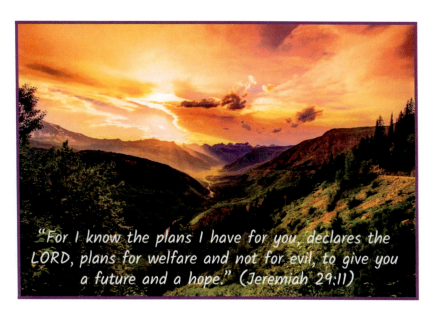

"For I know the plans I have for you, declares the LORD, plans for welfare and not for evil, to give you a future and a hope." (Jeremiah 29:11)

A peaceful feeling washes over me as read this verse. I am only one of billions of people on this planet. In spite of that, God has plans for me—specifically—to prosper me and to give me hope and a future. I matter to Him. I am grateful He has my future planned, that it is a good future, and I need not worry about tomorrow.

Whatever problems may surface today, I have confidence. I'm grateful Jesus has my back. Today I'm grateful for a call from a distant friend. **What are you grateful for today?**

_____

_____

_____

Vicki Andree

He Quiets Me

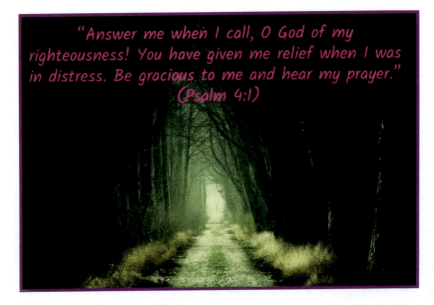

"Answer me when I call, O God of my righteousness! You have given me relief when I was in distress. Be gracious to me and hear my prayer." (Psalm 4:1)

My heart races in times of stress; the LORD hears me when I pray and ask for relief. He frees me from anxiety, helps me when I feel trapped, and protects me every day. He liberates me from those who want to harm me. He gives me peace and my heart relaxes into it's normal rhythm.

I'm grateful for His peace, the peace that passes all understanding. Today I'm grateful for new buds on the tree outside my office window. **What are you grateful for today?**

He Chooses The Time

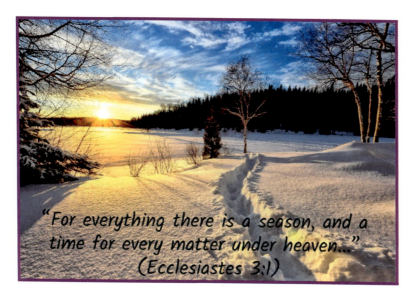

"For everything there is a season, and a time for every matter under heaven...."
(Ecclesiastes 3:1)

Sometimes I fail to understand why things happen when they do. As I contemplate this, I must admit that I do not have control over much. "A time to be born, and a time to die; a time to plant, and a time to pluck up what is planted; a time to kill, and a time to heal; a time to break down, and a time to build up; a time to weep, and a time to laugh; a time to mourn, and a time to dance..." God chooses the times; I choose how to respond.

I'm grateful that no matter the time, He is always with me. Today I'm grateful for my Bible study sisters. **What are you grateful for today?**

Vicki Andree

He Renews My Strength

The ESV says "wait" on the Lord; other versions say those who "trust" or "hope" in the LORD shall renew their strength. While I wait, trust, and hope in the LORD, He gives me strength like the eagles. Noted for their strong muscular legs and powerful talons, eagles rule the bird kingdom. Their exceptional vision enables them to hunt their prey from high above. Other birds of prey always glance behind them before striking their prey, eagles do not. They fear no other predator.

I am grateful that I do not need to fear what's behind me or ahead of me because the LORD has given me wings like the eagles. Today I'm grateful that spring has arrived. **What are you grateful for today?**

_____

_____

_____

He Restores Me

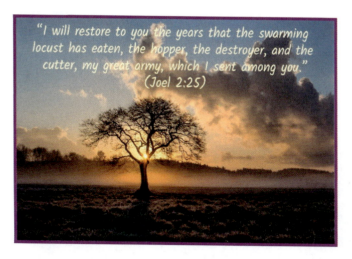

For many years this was my life verse. I clutched it, white knuckled, as I watched my life go up in flames. A combination of bad decisions and being in the wrong place at the right time increased my losses. At my lowest point, I knew in my heart that the LORD would keep His promise. I remember then having an unexplainable peace. The LORD kept His promise. He not only restored the years; He magnified what He repaid beyond what I could have ever thought or imagined. God keeps His promises.

    I am grateful for the years the LORD has restored. Today I am grateful for a great cooking tip from my sister in Nebraska. **What are you grateful for today?**

_____

_____

_____

He Delights Me

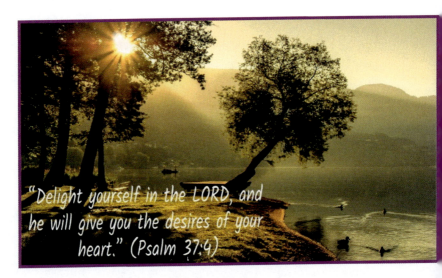

"Delight yourself in the LORD, and he will give you the desires of your heart." (Psalm 37:4)

Delighting in the LORD used to be one of my favorite things. I would sing praise songs and read favorite Scriptures to Him. I truly believed that in this way I would get what my heart desired. I admit it was pretty shallow. As my relationship with Jesus deepened, I found my desires changing. Jesus taught me that His desires and my desires should be alike. Delighting in Him meant desiring more of Him and less of me, this truth has drawn us closer than ever before.

I am grateful for the desires He has put in my heart. Such desires are pure, lovely, and glorify my Savior. Today I am grateful for my hard working, loving husband. **What are you grateful for today?**

I'm grateful for...

_____

_____

_____

His Mysterious Ways

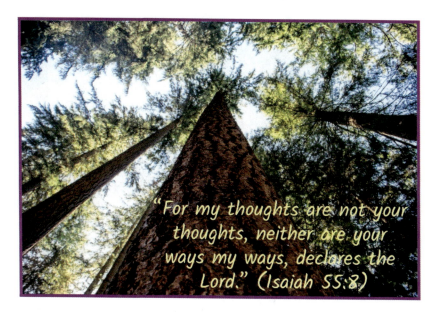

"For my thoughts are not your thoughts, neither are your ways my ways, declares the Lord." (Isaiah 55:8)

Every time I think I have God figured out, He surprises me. Often when I pray, I have an idea of how God will answer or solve the problem. Most of my ideas make perfect sense in this natural world. But God lives in a supernatural dimension and my ideas repeatedly fall short. His solutions are always better than anything I could ever devise.

I am grateful for my King of Kings, Lord of Lords, who found a way to deliver me from my sins and give me a future. Today I am grateful for lunch out with my son. **What are you grateful for today?**

_____

_____

_____

He Protects Me

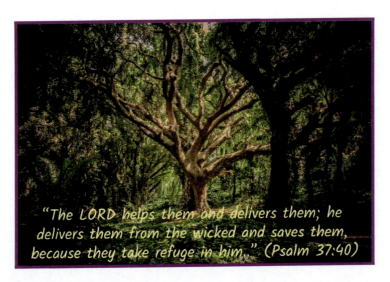

"The LORD helps them and delivers them; he delivers them from the wicked and saves them, because they take refuge in him." (Psalm 37:40)

Whenever I feel threatened, I run to the LORD. I ran to Him when my husband was unconscious for three days after emergency surgery. Proverbs 18:10 says, "The name of the LORD is a strong tower; the righteous man runs into it and is safe." I can only claim righteousness through Jesus, and I know God honors that. I can trust Him to protect and provide for me. So when trouble threatens and the wicked attack, I run to Him.

    I am grateful for God's loving protection throughout my day and in every situation. Today I am grateful to visit my granddaughters' school for grandparent's day. *What are you grateful for today?*

_____

_____

_____

He Lifts Me Up

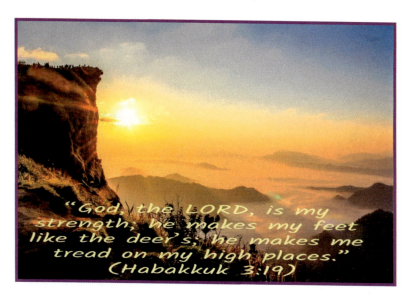

"God, the LORD, is my strength, he makes my feet like the deer's; he makes me tread on my high places." (Habakkuk 3:19)

The deer is a symbol of power, sensitivity, and gentleness. The stag is noted as the king of the forest and protector of all the other creatures in the forest. A deer is sure-footed with the ability to ascend to elevated places. I often see them on mountain passes as I drive to Steamboat Springs, Colorado. Sometimes they turn and leap over a fence or across a ditch, stretching muscles beneath shimming coats.

 I am grateful for the gifts of power, sensitivity, and gentleness granted by the LORD. He escorts me to high places. Today I am grateful for this sunny day. *What are you grateful for today?*

His Abundance

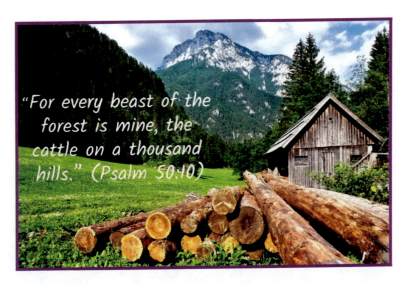

God owns more than the cattle on a thousand hills. He owns everything! It's all His. The LORD challenged me twice to raise funds, first to the mission in Malawi and then, a year later, the intended Bible School in Malawi. The enormous amount required to cover supplies, training, travel, shipping and customs seemed impossible. However, my God stepped in and miraculously provided everything we needed in record time! Everything is His. He decides when and where to distribute it.

I am grateful the LORD answered my prayer for support for missions. He always comes through. Today I am grateful for angel food cake and pineapple. *What are you grateful for today?*

He Rejoices Over Me

Wherever we are, the LORD is in the center. We can be grateful because His intent is not to harm or to judge, but to save us. He is so excited, so joyful at the prospect of saving you that He overflows with delight. In Hebrews it says that He suffered on the cross "for the joy set before Him." He rejoices over us and even sings loudly over us! His song resonates throughout my body, soul, and spirit.

I am grateful for God rejoicing at being in the center of my life. Today I am grateful for a roof over my head and a working furnace. **What are you grateful for today?**

_____

_____

_____

He Surrounds Me

"You hem me in, behind and before, and lay your hand upon me." (Psalm 139:5)

Some people have issues with being closed in. To feel surrounded by someone or something can be terrifying. In battle, to be hemmed in by the enemy is sure defeat. For believers, being hemmed in by the LORD is pure victory. Psalm 139 reveals that there is no place one can hide from God. He surrounds us.

    I am so very grateful that the LORD surrounds me. He is in me and through me and all around me every hour of every day. Today I am grateful for a myriad of good books. **What are you grateful for today?**

_____

_____

_____

His Desire For Me

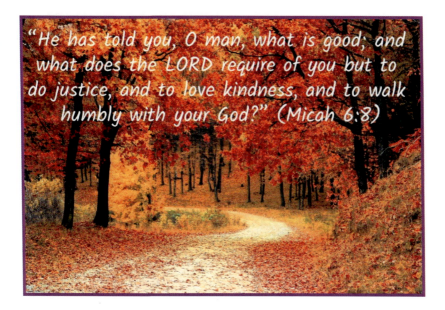

People often wonder what the LORD requires of us and this verse clearly explains His desire. None of this seems difficult, but I often make things harder than they need to be. My God created the universe and everything in it. Surely He deserves more than this verse states. But then again, I am human and even this is sometimes difficult to accomplish.

    I am grateful for His understanding when I fail to do justice, love kindness and walk humbly with Him. Today I am grateful for my stationary bike. ***What are you grateful for today?***

_____

_____

_____

He Fights For Me

"Contend, O LORD, with those who contend with me; fight against those who fight against me! (Psalm 35:1)

Years ago I found myself up against men in my office who wanted to harm me. They opposed any progress or ideas I suggested and constantly made fun of my efforts to do well. One day they fired me. I started my own company and the company that fired me went bankrupt. God fought for me and I actually got to see justice. Often we don't see justice, but God is fighting for us.

I am grateful that God let me see His justice on those that wronged me. He is faithful in all things. Today I am grateful for corn bags my sister made to keep my feet warm at night. *What are you grateful for today?*

_____

_____

_____

He Promised

The rainbow is a beautiful sight. Often we see it after a refreshing rain with green terrain beneath it. The first rainbow appeared after Noah exited the ark. At that time God told him that the rainbow would remind Him of His promise to never destroy the earth by water again. Since then there have been many floods, but never one to destroy the entire world.

I am grateful for God's promise to never destroy the world again with water. I am even more grateful for the LORD who keeps His promises. Today I am grateful for my pastor and for Christian radio. *What are you grateful for today?*

_____

_____

_____

He Cultivates Me

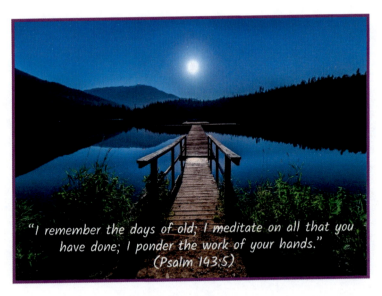

"I remember the days of old; I meditate on all that you have done; I ponder the work of your hands." (Psalm 143:5)

As I reflect on the chapters of my life I see how the LORD has painstakingly cultivated me to become the person I am today, continually being refined as gold or silver. Not every season seemed beneficial, but the LORD used the questionable times to educate me. Every experience, good or bad, He used for good. Some experiences are still maturing. Everything He creates is good.

I am grateful for all the experiences He has walked through with me. In each one He taught me more about His grace. Today I am grateful for the Bible and Bible translators. ***What are you grateful for today?***

He Walks With Me

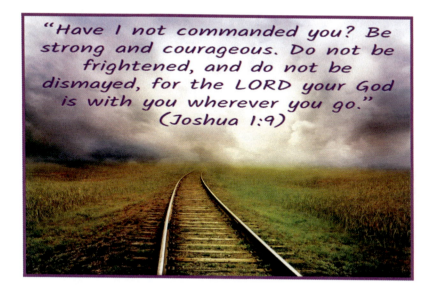

Often I can't see what's ahead and that can scare me. Instead of shaking in my boots, I try to take the next step. Always advancing and never stepping back, always trusting by remembering this verse. Whenever I must shake off fear, I remember that fear is False Evidence Appearing Real, that God is real, and that He is with me wherever I go. He walks ahead of me and clears the way.

    I am grateful that God walks with me wherever I go. I need not be frightened. Today I am grateful for good advice from my sister in Kansas. ***What are you grateful for today?***

_____

_____

_____

He Bestows Wisdom

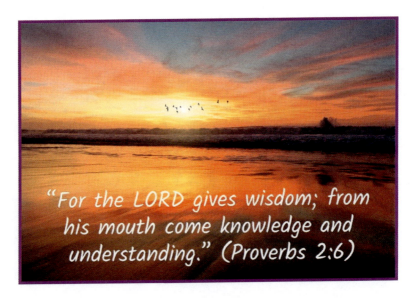

"For the LORD gives wisdom; from his mouth come knowledge and understanding." (Proverbs 2:6)

Wisdom is valuable. King Solomon asked for wisdom and he became the wisest, richest man in the world. People from all around came to him for advice. My life-long quest for wisdom has yielded a myriad of benefits, not as impressive as King Solomon's, but every bit as appreciated. You see, the LORD is the source of wisdom. The more wisdom, knowledge and understanding you receive, the closer you move toward God.

I am grateful that through prayer, study, experiences, and faith God has granted me a measure of wisdom. Today I am grateful for my grandson, even if he is a teenager. ***What are you grateful for today?***

He Arranges Divine Appointments

The story of Esther keeps me on the edge of my seat until Esther overcomes the threat from Haman. From Esther I learned the phrase, "For such a time as this." Knowing God has my days planned and numbered encourages me to keep watch for divine appointments. All of those "coincidental" happenings are planned by God. Through them I have opportunity to further the kingdom.

I am grateful for the story of Esther. It reminds me to be ready with an answer for my hope. Today I am grateful for my computer, even through it sometimes upsets me. ***What are you grateful for today?***

_____

_____

_____

He Increases My Days

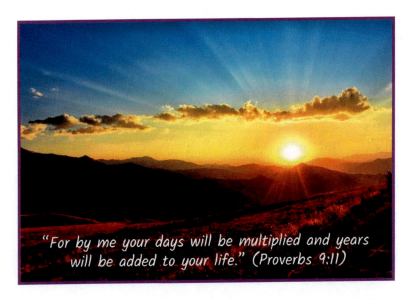

"For by me your days will be multiplied and years will be added to your life." (Proverbs 9:11)

This verse is about wisdom. A wise person accepts criticism and learns from it. A wise person is teachable. Verse 10 says, "The fear of the LORD is the beginning of wisdom, and the knowledge of the Holy One is insight." Fear of the LORD brings health, enduring wealth, and peace. God approves of 'fear of the LORD' and by Him my days will multiplied. Fear also means awe, respect and love.

    I am grateful to be alive. I am grateful for the hard days which make the good days even better. Today I am grateful that I grew up in a small town. ***What are you grateful for today?***

_____

_____

_____

He Feeds Me

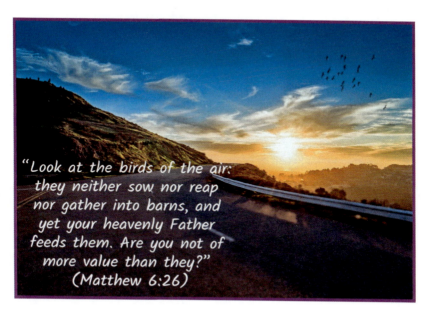

"Look at the birds of the air: they neither sow nor reap nor gather into barns, and yet your heavenly Father feeds them. Are you not of more value than they?" (Matthew 6:26)

My bird feeders always need filling. Some days I see so many little sparrows I wonder where they all come from. When I think about the LORD watching over each one of them, I remember this verse and bear in mind that this message is for me. I can stop worrying about what to eat or what to wear. My heavenly Father takes care of me in every way.

I am grateful for little sparrows that remind me of a God who cares about every little thing going on in my life. Today I am grateful for an abundance of food and clean water. ***What are you grateful for today?***

_____

_____

_____

His Peace Shields Me

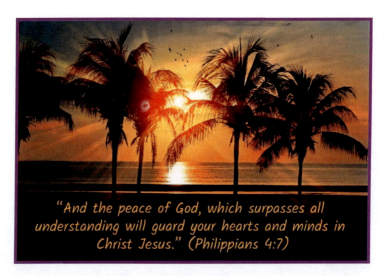

"And the peace of God, which surpasses all understanding will guard your hearts and minds in Christ Jesus." (Philippians 4:7)

Perfect peace comes only from God. It is not based on a psychological state of mind, good feelings, or nonexistent conflict. I can't think of anyone who lives in perfect peace. Most people I know would settle for any peace. I live in such an age of activity and strife that I often pray for the peace 'which surpasses all understanding.' Immediately, I feel a shield raise up between me and the cares of this world.

    I am grateful that in this busy world of constant conflict, I can lift my concerns to Jesus and He will extend perfect peace. Today I am grateful for the man who came to help clean up my back yard. ***What are you grateful for today?***

_____

_____

_____

He Calms My Storms

"And he awoke and rebuked the wind and said to the sea, 'Peace! Be still!' And the wind ceased, and there was great calm." (Mark 4:39)

When I can't go to sleep at night, I think of Jesus asleep in a small boat being tossed about in a storm. Sleeping at a time like that accentuates His confidence. The disciples woke Him up and He calmed the storm. This verse reminds me that Jesus is the Creator and Sustainer of the universe. Even nature is subject to His command. When He says "Peace! Be Still!" there is peace and the waters are stilled.

When I am battling a storm, I cry out to Jesus. He hears me and calms the storm. I am grateful for peace in the middle of the storm. Today I am grateful to live in the USA. **What are you grateful for today?**

_____

_____

_____

Vicki Andree

He Fulfills The Impossible

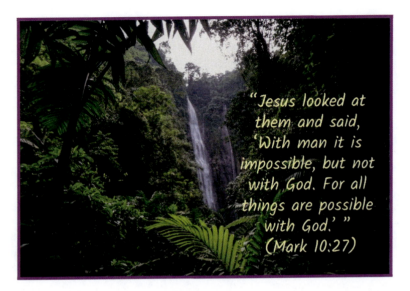

"Jesus looked at them and said, 'With man it is impossible, but not with God. For all things are possible with God.'" (Mark 10:27)

Have you ever been in a group where everyone said your goal was impossible to meet? When I look back at certain times in my life, I cannot believe all I achieved. In fact, if someone had ordered me to perform all those tasks, I would have said it was impossible. Only by the hand of God did I carry out my goals. God makes the impossible possible! Moses stuttered, but God used him to deliver His people.

I try to take one day at a time, one task at a time and keep moving. I am grateful that with God all things are possible. Today I am grateful for sidewalks and playgrounds. **What are you grateful for today?**

He Increases My Faith

"Truly, I say to you, whoever says to this mountain, 'Be taken up and thrown into the sea,' and does not doubt in his heart, but believes what he says will come to pass, it will be done for him." (Mark 11:23)

Resilient faith can overcome many obstacles. Jesus used the example of moving a mountain to emphasize just how powerful faith can be. I believe everyone is given a measure of faith. Increasing faith is an exercise in trusting God. I pray, believing and trusting He will answer. He responds. My faith increases.

I am grateful for the mountain of faith God bestowed upon me. Faith gets me through the bad days and makes the good days even better. Today I am grateful my car is fixed. ***What are you grateful for today?***

_____

_____

_____

Vicki Andree

He Forgives Me

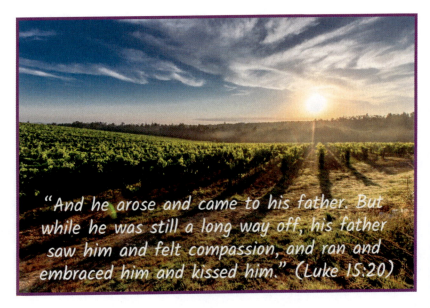

"And he arose and came to his father. But while he was still a long way off, his father saw him and felt compassion, and ran and embraced him and kissed him." (Luke 15:20)

This is the story of the Prodigal Son, but it's also a picture of God's forgiveness and love for us. He gave us free will, and at times we misuse that gift. We fall away, but He waits patiently for our repentance so we can return to our Father. He not only forgives, but welcomes us with open arms.

I am so grateful for God's forgiveness. He never remembers our sin, but casts it as far as the east is from the west. Today I am grateful for good neighbors. **What are you grateful for today?**

_____

_____

_____

He Frees Me

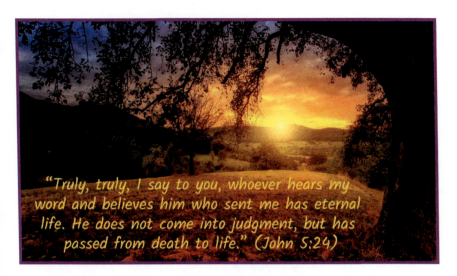

"Truly, truly, I say to you, whoever hears my word and believes him who sent me has eternal life. He does not come into judgment, but has passed from death to life." (John 5:24)

Whoever hears His word and believes in Jesus has eternal life. My eternal life began the moment I accepted Jesus Christ as my Lord and Savior because from now to forever I am living with Jesus. He freed me from the burden of judgment and assures me that I will be with Him in heaven one day. There is no greater gift than this: that Christ laid His life down for me. His death on the cross freed me.

I am eternally grateful for the sacrifice Jesus made to free me from sin and death. Today I am grateful for good, clean movies and popcorn. **What are you grateful for today?**

_____

_____

_____

He Keeps Me Forever

"All that the Father gives me will come to me, and whoever comes to me I will never cast out." John 6:37

Jesus will never turn me away. Not only that, I can send anyone I meet to Him and He will not turn them away. Yes, all of us must repent and accept Him as Lord and Savior, but when we do that we are assured of an eternity with Him in heaven. He will never change His mind. We belong to Him and we receive His blessings forever.

Only Jesus can give us the blessed life. He wants us to come to Him. I am grateful that I belong to Him forever. Today I am grateful for the LORD's missionaries. ***What are you grateful for today?***

I'm grateful for...

_____

_____

_____

He Is Love

"A new commandment I give to you, that you love one another: just as I have loved you, you also are to love one another." (John 13:34)

Some people think that the definition of love is subjective. Not true. God is love. Jesus commanded that we love one another just as He loved us. Think about what that means. He loved us so much that He submitted Himself to humiliation, torment, torture, and death at the hands of the enemy. He made the ultimate sacrifice so I could live.

    I show gratitude for His love by loving my neighbor. Who is my neighbor? Everyone around me. I am grateful to experience true love. Today I am grateful for my soft, comfy blanket. **What are you grateful for today?**

I'm grateful for...

_____

_____

_____

He Offers Me The Kingdom

My God is generous. He has the right to offer me a kingdom that cannot be shaken. I accept the offer with thanksgiving. Therefore, I make it a point to worship Him at church, in my home, and wherever I happen to be. I say grace in public. I praise Him all day. Yes, I am in awe that the Creator of the universe chose me. When He speaks, I reverently bow.

I am grateful to be part of the family of God and for receiving the holy kingdom that cannot be shaken. Today I am grateful for shoes that feel good. *What are you grateful for today?*

_____

_____

_____

His Power Overcomes

"Submit yourselves therefore to God. Resist the devil, and he will flee from you." (James 4:7)

I have a healthy understanding of the devil; he hates me and wants to steal my joy. He tried to destroy the world. Jesus defeated him at the cross. The devil knows his days are short so he wants to make me miserable. Fortunately, I have a close relationship with Jesus. I submitted my life to Him long ago. Whenever the devil comes around, I start praising God for putting my feet on solid ground.

I am grateful Jesus overcame the evil one at the cross and continues to hold him at bay. I can submit and resist. Thank You, Lord! Today I am grateful for good eyesight. *What are you grateful for today?*

_____

_____

_____

Vicki Andree

He Offers New Life

"We were buried therefore with him by baptism into death, in order that, just as Christ was raised from the dead by the glory of the Father, we too might walk in newness of life." (Romans 6:4)

I confess. I've been baptized three times. Once when I was twelve. Again when I was an adult; a rededication of my life. And finally in the Jordan River in Israel; I couldn't resist being baptized in the same water Jesus was baptized in. The symbolism means buried with Christ and raised up out of the water to walk in a new life.

I am grateful for each time I submitted to baptism. I don't want one day to pass that I don't remember the death, burial, and resurrection of Jesus Christ. I am grateful for my new life. Today I am grateful for hearing aids. ***What are you grateful for today?***

His Incredible Fruit

No one can match the generosity of God. He gives us all kinds of different gifts, but the fruit of the Spirit is given to every believer. Every one of us have the capacity to love. All of the gifts are beneficial in all areas of our lives. He came so that we could have abundant lives. These gifts make anyone richer. A beautiful aspect of this fruit of the Spirit is that none of it is illegal so no one can take it away!

I am grateful for the generosity of God. I'm grateful for the fruit of Spirit that can never be taken away. Today I am grateful for beautiful trees and flowers. ***What are you grateful for today?***

_____

_____

_____

He Satisfies

Contentment is one of those things that's hard to find in this society. When I meet a happy person, they are usually contented. They don't have a lot of hang-ups about changing things or having the next newest release of whatever. They are relaxed and seem to enjoy life more than others. It is good to be content with what God is doing in our lives.

I'm grateful for the days I feel contented. Sometimes I forget that God is in control, but for the most part I'm content. Today I am grateful for the view of the mountains from my kitchen window. ***What are you grateful for today?***

_____

_____

_____

His Grace

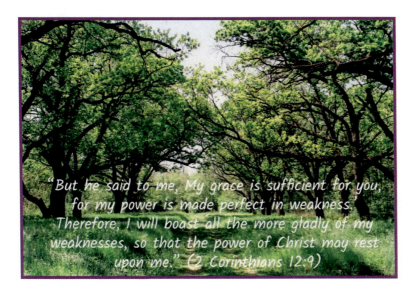

"But he said to me, My grace is sufficient for you, for my power is made perfect in weakness.' Therefore, I will boast all the more gladly of my weaknesses, so that the power of Christ may rest upon me." (2 Corinthians 12:9)

Grace is my favorite word. God's grace abounds. He is generous with it. I like the acronym G.R.A.C.E. — God's riches at Christ's expense. When I am weak, God's strength is apparent. When I miraculously finish an impossible task, I know it was accomplished by God's power. I am happy to give the LORD credit, because without Him I am nothing.

I am grateful of the unending grace of God. Let me be weak so I can show His strength. I love to experience God's power. Today I am grateful for walks on the beach and sunshine. *What are you grateful for today?*

I'm grateful for...

_____

_____

_____

He Encourages Me

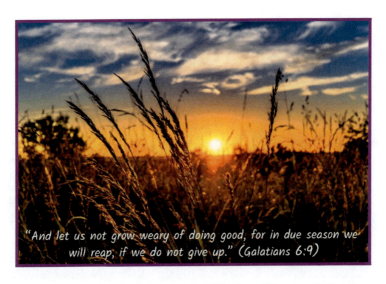

"And let us not grow weary of doing good, for in due season we will reap, if we do not give up." (Galatians 6:9)

Jesus gave Christians one last command before He ascended to heaven. "Go therefore and make disciples of all nations, baptizing them in the name of the Father and of the Son and of the Holy Spirit..." (Matthew 28:19). Doing good softens hard soil so others can plant. Like many of you, I sometimes wonder if I am making any progress. This verse reminds me to persist in my efforts even when I don't see progress.

I am grateful for this reminder that in due season we will see results. One may sow and another reap. We are all one body, serving one God. Today I am grateful for beautiful sculptures and paintings. ***What are you grateful for today?***

He Focuses On My Future

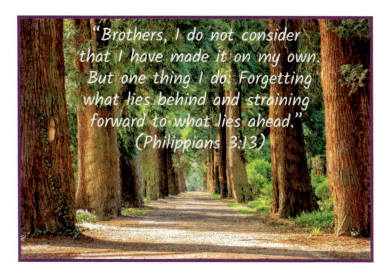

"Brothers, I do not consider that I have made it on my own. But one thing I do: Forgetting what lies behind and straining forward to what lies ahead." (Philippians 3:13)

If I ponder my past too long, I realize that the evil one is at it again, trying to steal my joy. Instead of dwelling on past mistakes, I look forward to a future of enjoying the ultimate privilege — serving God. I look forward to a closer relationship with Jesus as He teaches me about His desires for me. I long to be the woman He created me to be. No regrets here, only incredible, unbridled freedom in Christ knowing that what lies ahead is better than I can imagine.

    I gratefully look forward with anticipation to each day. As it unfolds, I see God at work all around me. Today I am grateful for my loving brother and road trips. ***What are you grateful for today?***

_____

_____

_____

He Teaches Me

"Finally, brothers, whatever is true, whatever is honorable, whatever is just, whatever is pure, whatever is lovely, whatever is commendable, if there's any excellence, if there is anything worthy of praise, think about these things." (Philippians 4:8)

This is another of my favorite verses. Adopting this attitude in my thoughts frees me from judging, depression, and gossip. So I ask myself. Is this true? Is it honorable? Is it just? Is it pure? Is it lovely, commendable, excellent, or praise worthy? If it isn't, it's time to change the subject. I don't always succeed, but I keep trying and I keep getting better at it! I've found it's just a matter of paying attention and corralling my thoughts.

I am grateful for a verse that teaches me how to discipline my mind so my actions will glorify the LORD. Today I am grateful for my kitchen appliances. ***What are you grateful for today?***

He Completes Me

"And I am sure of this, that he who began a good work in you will bring it to completion at the day of Jesus Christ." (Philippians 1:6)

Sometimes I feel like I'm not growing. Sometimes my spiritual life seems flat and my prayers don't seem as intense as they should. I know the LORD is near, but sometimes I can't feel His presence. That's when I turn to this verse which reminds me that Jesus is still working on me. He will not quit or give up on me until He has completed the good work He started.

I am grateful that God is not finished with me yet. He will continue working on me until I meet Him in heaven. Today I am grateful for my space heater. *What are you grateful for today?*

_____

_____

_____

He Is Greater

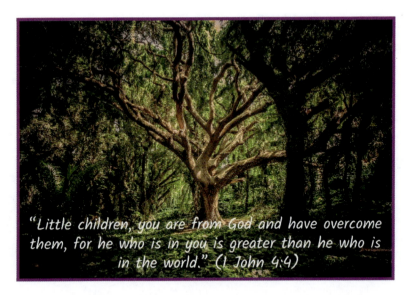

"Little children, you are from God and have overcome them, for he who is in you is greater than he who is in the world." (1 John 4:4)

All authority in heaven and on earth has been given to Jesus Christ by the Father. The devil is a fallen angel. He and Jesus have never been equal at any time. In fact, Jesus created angels, therefore, He is high above them. The devil wants me to think he has power, but since I have the Holy Spirit sent from Jesus in me, I have power from Jesus. Greater is He who in me!

I am grateful for the Holy Spirit in me, who is greater than the evil one or his agents, human or spiritual. Today I am grateful for rainy days. **What are you grateful for today?**

Conclusion

I hope that now you are counting your blessings more often. Just a quick prayer of thanksgiving each evening pleases our LORD and Savior. He is worthy of praise and thanksgiving. In fact, only He is worthy.

I have found that the more I express my gratitude to Jesus, the more I find myself blessed. Most days I find it difficult to count the number of blessings!

It has been a pleasure spending the last forty days with you as we expressed gratitude for the many blessings Jesus poured out on us. I will continue to thank Him, and I hope you will too. ***What are you grateful for today?***

Books by Vicki Andree

Devotionals
- The Miracle of You
- El Milagro de Ti
- Attitude Matters
- La Actitud Importa
- Gratitude: A 40 Day Adventure

Personal Experience
- On Our Own In Jerusalem's Old City

Bible Study
- Misunderstood

Inspirational Christian Fiction
- Lyza's Story - Book One of The Lane Trilogy
- The Legacy - Book Two of the Lane Trilogy
- Leesa's Story - Book Three of the Lane Trilogy
- I Hate Walt
- I Hate Walt, Too: The Sequel

Made in the USA
Middletown, DE
28 May 2024